W9-AUI-575

Social Studies Alive!®
My School and Family

TCi™

Chief Executive Officer: Bert Bower
Chief Operating Officer: Amy Larson
Director of Product Development: Liz Russell
Managing Editor: Laura Alavosus
Editorial Project Manager: Lara Fox
Project Editor: Beverly Cory
Editorial Associates: Anna Embree and Sarah Sudano
Production Manager: Lynn Sanchez
Design Manager: Jeff Kelly
Graphic Designer: Cheri DeBusk
Photo Edit Manager: Margee Robinson
Photo Editor: Diane Austin
Art Editor: Sarah Wildfang
Audio Manager: Katy Haun

TCi™ Teachers' Curriculum Institute
PO Box 50996
Palo Alto, CA 94303

Customer Service: 800-497-6138
www.teachtci.com

ISBN 978-1-58371-776-9
1 2 3 4 5 6 7 8 9 10 WC 15 14 13 12 11 10 09

Program Director
Bert Bower

Program Consultant
Vicki LaBoskey, Ph.D., Professor of
Education, Mills College, Oakland,
California

Student Edition Writers
Laura M. Alavosus
Abigail Boyce
Susan Buckley
Beverly Cory
Wendy Frey

Curriculum Developers
Joyce Bartky
Nicolle Hutchinson

Reading Specialist
Barbara Schubert, Ph.D., Reading
Specialist, Saint Mary's College,
Moraga, California

Teacher and Content Consultants
Jill Bartky, Teacher, Sharp Park
Elementary School, Pacifica, California

Debra Elsen, Teacher, Manchester
Elementary, Manchester, Maryland

Gina Frazzini, Literary Coach, Gatzert
Elementary, Seattle, Washington

Patrick J. Lee, Teacher, Ohlone
Elementary, Palo Alto, California

Jennifer Miley, Teacher, Duveneck
Elementary School, Palo Alto, California

Mitch Pascal, Social Studies Specialist,
Arlington County Schools, Arlington,
Virginia

Jodi Perraud, Teacher, Boulevard Heights
Elementary, Hollywood, Florida

Becky Suthers, Retired Teacher, Stephen
F. Austin Elementary, Weatherford, Texas

Literature Consultant
Regina M. Rees, Ph.D., Assistant
Professor, Beeghly College of Education,
Youngstown State University,
Youngstown, Ohio

Music Specialist
Beth Yankee, Teacher, The Woodward
School for Technology and Research,
Kalamazoo, Michigan

Maps
Mapping Specialists, Ltd. Madison,
Wisconsin

Contents

Maps

How Do We Get Along in School?

New Ideas

share

talk

listen

take turns

1.1 We Share

We get along by sharing. We share because we often like to do the same things. It feels good to share with our friends! What do we share?

1.2 We Talk

We get along by talking. We may be unhappy or angry. We talk about our feelings. That helps others to understand us. Then we can get along better. When do we talk to others?

1.3 We Listen

We get along by listening. We listen to our friends. They tell us their feelings. They tell us their ideas. We listen to our teacher, too. How do we listen?

1.4 We Take Turns

We get along by taking turns. When we take turns, we each get to do something we like to do. When do we take turns?

Summary

Here are some ways we get along. We share. We talk. We listen. We take turns. What else can we do to get along?

7

A Place to Share

Neighbors in New York City had a problem. They had to work it out. How do people get along in a city?

Mary Foster lives in New York City. She loves to garden. Where could she have a garden in the big city?

Mrs. Foster saw a vacant lot on her block. People left trash there.

Mrs. Foster cleaned up the lot. Her children, Sparkle and Starr, helped. Then, they planted a garden.

People on the block liked the garden. Mrs. Foster said, "We can share. The garden is for all of us."

One day, Mrs. Foster found a lock on the garden gate. She learned that the city owned the lot. And the city wanted to sell it. That would be the end of her garden.

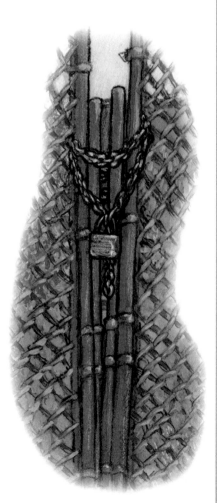

People were upset. They loved the garden. They met and talked. Should they let the city sell the lot? Or should they try to save the garden?

Many people spoke up. They talked about what the garden meant to them. The city listened.

By working together, the people saved Mrs. Foster's garden. Today, the garden has a name. It is the Mo' Pals Community Garden.

Young and old people share this space. It is like a park. People plant things. They weed. They grow good things to eat. The garden is a happy place to share.

Why Is It Important to Learn from Each Other?

New Ideas

alike

different

learn

2.1 Each of Us Is Special

We are all alike in some ways.

We are different in some ways, too.

Each of us is special. What makes

you special?

2.2 We Are Good at Different Things

Some of us are good at drawing.

Some of us are good at counting. Some

of us are good at singing. What things

can you do well?

2.3 You Can Learn from Me

I can help you learn new things.
I can catch a baseball. I can do magic
tricks. What would you like to learn
from me?

2.4 I Can Learn from You

You can help me learn new things.

I want to learn how to play the drums.

I want to learn how to make a puppet.

What would you like to help me learn?

Summary

Each of us is special. We are good at different things. You can learn from me. I can learn from you.

The Ant's Lesson

A grasshopper and an ant were good at different things. What can a grasshopper learn from an ant?

The sun was shining. It was a hot summer day. A grasshopper sang and danced. He loved making music.

An ant passed by. He was carrying corn to his nest. The ant was working very hard.

The grasshopper said, "Ant, why do you work so hard? Come and play!"

The ant said, "I am too busy. I am storing food for the winter. You should be storing food, too."

The grasshopper laughed. He nibbled a green leaf. "I have all the food that I need," he said. "Winter is far away. I want to have fun."

Summer passed. The ant spent his days working. He filled his nest with food for winter.

The grasshopper kept on playing his music. He danced and ate leaves all day long.

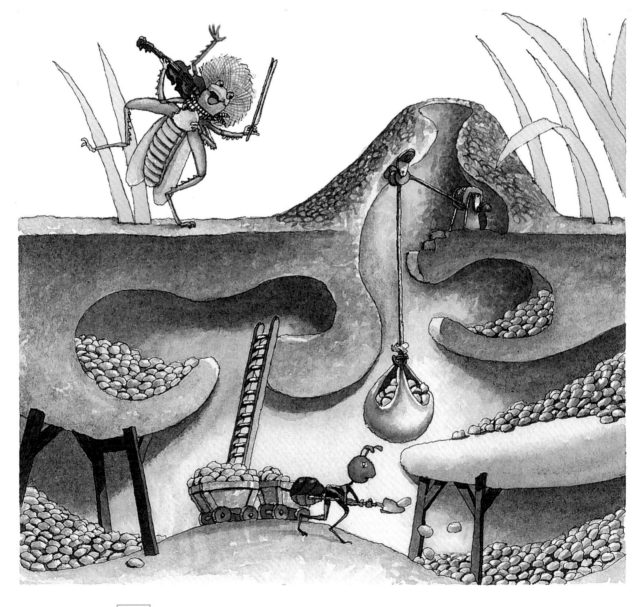

Then winter came. Snow fell. Food
was hard to find. The grasshopper was
so cold and hungry!

Down in their nest, the ants shared
the food they had stored all summer.

The grasshopper was very sad. If
only he had listened to the ant!

There is a time to work and a time
to play. Always think about tomorrow.

Please WALK with your tra

Why Do Schools Have Rules?

New Ideas

get along

be safe

be fair

learn

3.1 Rules Help Us Get Along

We need to get along at school. We are kind. We talk and listen to each other. We tell the truth. What else do we do to get along at school?

3.2 Rules Help Us Be Safe

We need to be safe at school. We line up. We don't run in the halls. We wait to cross the street. What else do we do to be safe at school?

25

3.3 Rules Help Us Be Fair

We need to be fair at school.
We share. We take turns. We let
everyone play. What else do we do
to be fair at school?

3.4 Rules Help Us Learn

We need to learn at school. We pay attention. We do our schoolwork. What else do we do to learn at school?

Summary

We need to get along. We need to be safe. We need to be fair. We need to learn. That is why schools have rules.

Let's Vote on It

Schools need rules. Towns and cities need rules, too. Who makes the rules in a city?

Some cities have rules like these:

- Dogs must be on a leash.

- Skateboards cannot be used on city streets.

- No one can set off fireworks.

In Bellflower, California, school classes take field trips to City Hall. They learn how the city makes rules.

Ms. Callahan took her class to City Hall. They acted out a city meeting. Each child had a part to play.

Some children were the city leaders. They sat at the big desk. Some played the part of people who live in the city.

In their meeting, the class talked about bike use. "Can we ride our bikes on the sidewalk?"

Some children said yes. The street is not safe for bikes. Some children said no. People walk on the sidewalk. Bikes might run into them. Someone said, "Let's build a bike lane."

The leaders talked. They said, "Let's vote on it!" Five leaders voted yes. Nobody voted no.

It would be a new rule. Anyone on a bike must use the bike lane. Then they voted for a second rule. They voted that children on bikes must wear helmets.

Of course, the children did not really make new rules for their city. But they learned how the city leaders make rules.

When they are 18, these children will have the right to vote. Then they can choose the real city leaders, who make the real rules.

Who Helps Us at School?

New Ideas

teacher

principal

secretary

custodian

4.1 A Teacher

I like to help children learn. I like to learn, too. I listen to children. I help children get along. I teach children new things. I help them with their work. Who am I?

34

4.2 A Principal

I am a leader. I like to help teachers and students. I like to help families. Every day, I help people solve problems. I am proud of my school. Who am I?

4.3 A Secretary

I work at my desk all day. I like to greet visitors. I like to help the principal. I like to help children, too.

I answer the phone.

I answer questions.

Who am I?

4.4 A Custodian

I like to keep our school clean.
I like to fix things. Sometimes I work
outdoors. I keep our school safe.
Who am I?

Summary

Lots of people help us at school. Teachers
help us. The principal helps us. The school
secretary and the custodian help us, too.

Ms. Johnson Has Many Jobs

This Texas woman is a leader in Congress. Her job is to help people. How does she help them?

Eddie Bernice Johnson

Eddie Bernice Johnson works in Washington, D.C. What are her jobs? She helps make laws. And she votes on how to spend the country's money.

Ms. Johnson visits a Texas school. She knows that reading helps children learn. She votes to spend money on books for poor children.

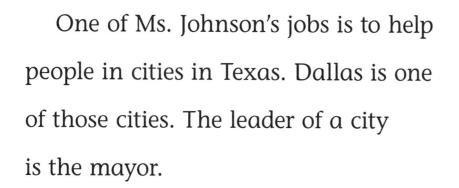

One of Ms. Johnson's jobs is to help people in cities in Texas. Dallas is one of those cities. The leader of a city is the mayor.

Ms. Johnson talked to the mayor of Dallas. They built new homes. People fixed the streets. They put in a new park. They made the city of Dallas a better place to live.

The Mayor

The Governor

Ms. Johnson also works with state leaders. It is her job to help the state of Texas. The state leader is the governor.

Some years, Texas gets too much rain. Then there are bad floods. Streets fill with water. Homes fill with mud. Ms. Johnson talks to the governor of Texas. They work together to help the people.

Ms. Johnson also works with the president. The president is the leader of the United States.

They talk about ways to help. How can we help people find jobs? How can we make schools better? How can we keep the air clean? They talk about all these things.

Eddie Bernice Johnson is a leader. She helps the people in her state. Who are the leaders in your state?

How Are We Good Helpers at School?

New Ideas

help others

take care of our things

do our best

respect others

5.1 We Help Others

We help others at school. We help the teacher clean up. We share books with friends. How else do we help each other?

5.2 We Take Care of Our Things

We take care of our things at school. We are careful with our crayons. We put the balls away after recess. How else do we take care of our things at school?

45

5.3 We Do Our Best

We do our best at school. We ask questions. We finish our work. We remember to line up for recess. How else do we do our best at school?

5.4 We Respect Others

We respect others at school. We say "please" and "thank you." We are good winners and losers. How else do we respect others at school?

Summary

We help others. We take care of our things. We do our best. We respect others.

Clara Barton Helped Others

Clara Barton lived a long time ago.

She had a gift for helping people.

How was she a good helper?

When Clara was a little girl, her brother was very sick. Clara stayed by his bed for two years. She watched the doctor. She learned what to do. She helped her brother get better.

For Clara, this was just a start. She would be a good helper all her life.

Clara loved school. When she grew
up, she took a job as a teacher. She
helped her class read maps. She helped
them read books. She treated her
students with respect.

In time, she opened her own school.
It was the first free school in New Jersey.
This gave poor children the chance to
go to school.

Then one year, Clara watched war break out. She saw men go off to fight.

Clara could see that the men needed help. They needed food. They needed clothing. Some were hurt.

Clara did her best to help. She worked as a nurse. She worked without pay. She was very brave. She helped save lives.

Later in her life, Clara started the American Red Cross.

The Red Cross helps people in need. It helps people who lose their homes in fires and bad storms. It gives them food, clothing, and a place to stay.

Do you know the Golden Rule? It says to treat others the way you would like to be treated. That is how Clara Barton lived her life.

What Is a Map?

New Ideas

map

symbol

map key

compass rose

direction

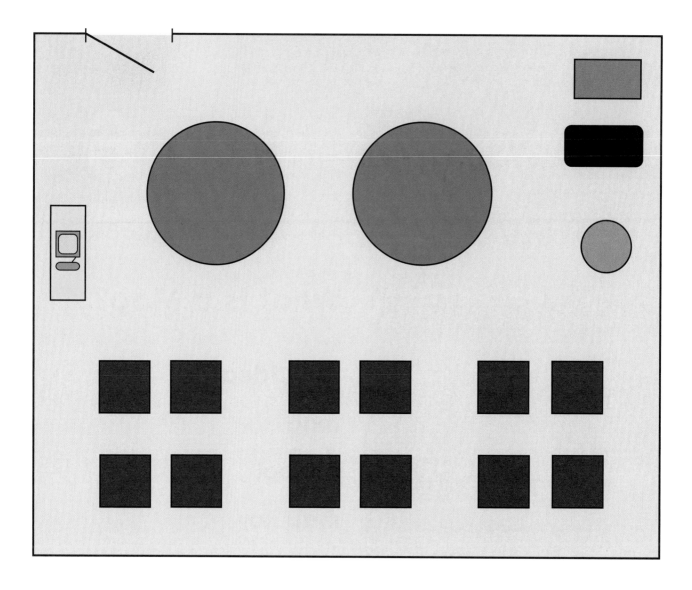

6.1 A Map Is a Drawing of a Place

A map shows what a place looks like from above. Some maps show countries. Some maps show cities. Some maps show rooms in buildings. What else do maps show?

6.2 A Map Has Symbols

Symbols are pictures that stand for objects. You can draw a circle for a table. You can draw a square for a desk. What other symbols can you draw?

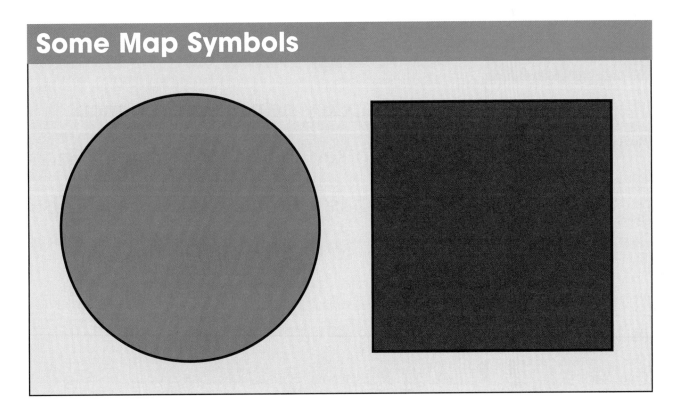

Some Map Symbols

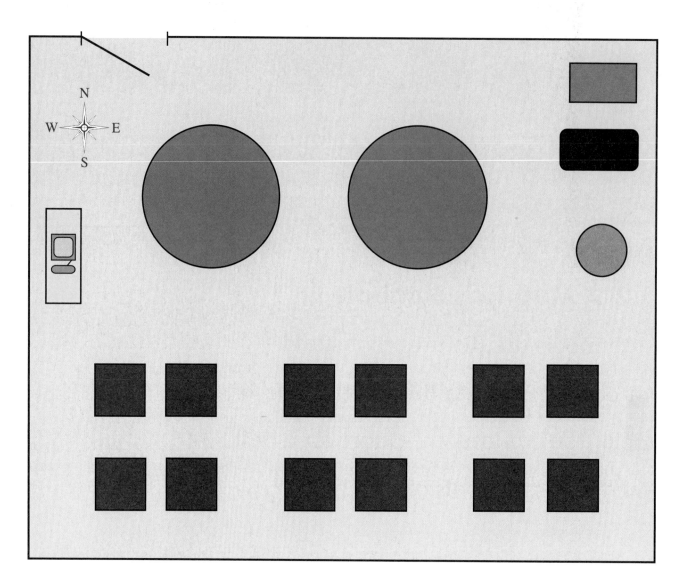

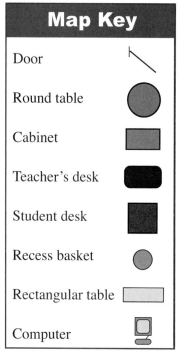

Map Key	
Door	
Round table	
Cabinet	
Teacher's desk	
Student desk	
Recess basket	
Rectangular table	
Computer	

6.3 A Map Has a Key

A map key helps us read a map. The map key shows each symbol. Each symbol has a name. Can you use this map key to find things on the map?

6.4 A Compass Rose Shows Directions

How do we show directions on a map? We use a compass rose. The four letters stand for the directions. N stands for north. S stands for south. E stands for east. W stands for west.

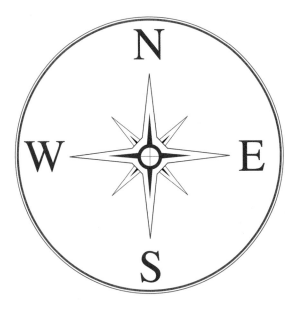

Summary

A map is a special drawing of a place. A map has symbols. A map key tells what the symbols mean. A compass rose shows directions.

The Right Kind of Map

There are all kinds of maps. Mr. Kelly's class went looking for a map. What kind of map was it?

Today we made a map of our school. Mr. Kelly gave us the outline and the words. We filled in the map.

Then Mr. Kelly said, "Who likes to ice skate?" We all stared at him. What does ice skating have to do with maps?

Computer lab
Multi-Use Room
Playground
Library
Nurse
Office

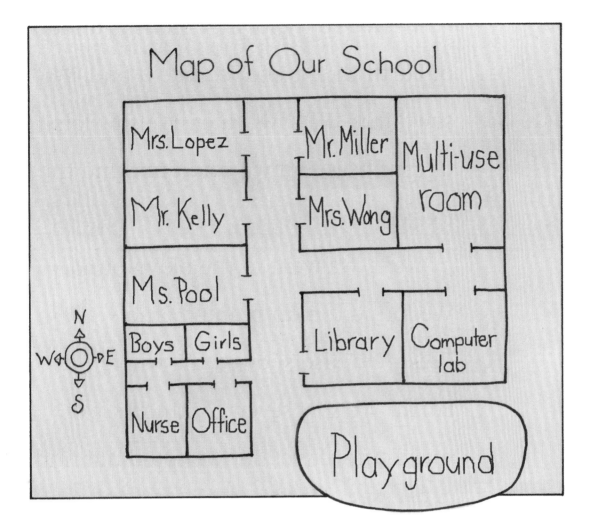

Map of Our School

"I will take the class ice skating," said Mr. Kelly. "But first, you have to find a map for me. We need a map that shows where the ice rink is. Here is a clue. The map is somewhere in our school."

So, we set off on a map hunt. First, we went to the library.

We found a globe. A globe is a map of Earth that is shaped like a ball. We saw land. We saw water. We saw lots of countries. But we could not find the ice rink.

Next, we went to the playground. We found a map painted on a wall. This map also showed the whole Earth. We saw seven continents. We saw four oceans. But we could not find the ice rink.

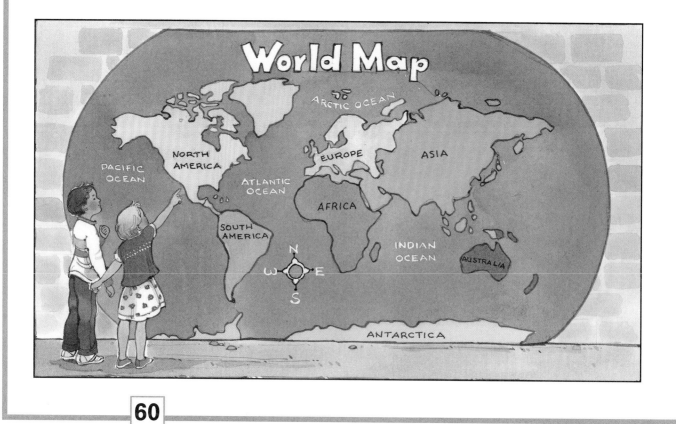

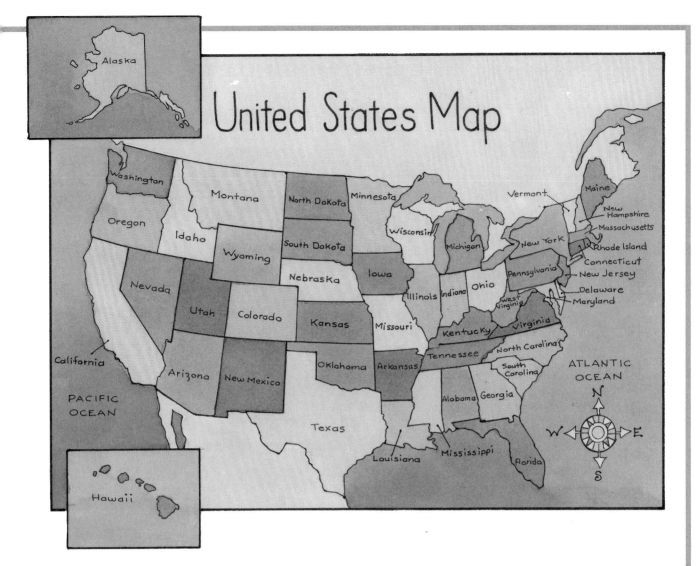

Next, we went to Mrs. Wong's room.

She had a map of the United States.

This map showed all 50 states.

We found our state. We saw the

Great Lakes. But we could not find

the ice rink.

Next, we went to the computer lab. There we found a big map of our state, Oregon.

We saw lots of mountains. We saw lakes. We saw rivers. We saw cities. But we still could not find the ice rink.

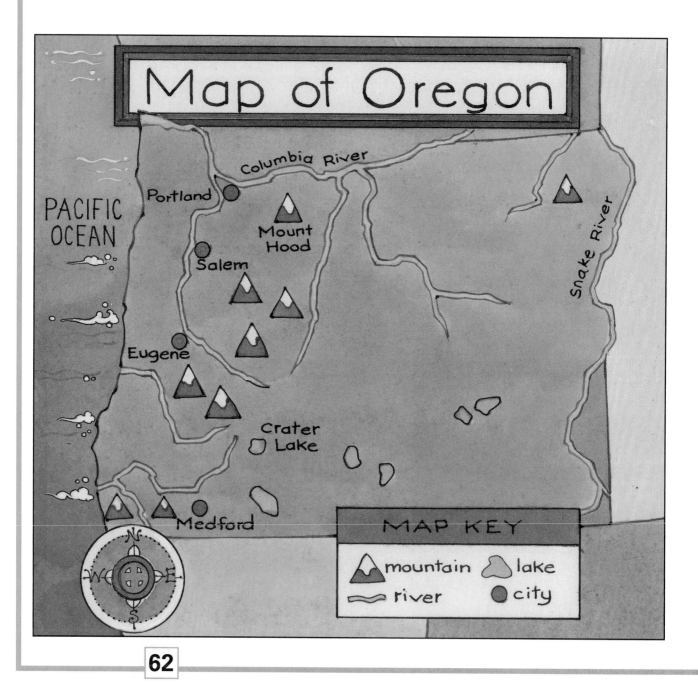

Map of Our Community

Our last stop was the school office.
We were ready to give up. Then, we
saw one more map. It showed our town.

We looked on all the streets. We
found our school. We found the park.
We found City Hall. And at last, we
found the ice rink.

"We did it, Mr. Kelly! Let's go
ice skating!"

What Was School Like Long Ago?

New Ideas

long ago

schoolhouse

hornbook

7.1 Schoolhouses Were Different

Long ago, a schoolhouse had one room. There was a big stove in the room for heating. The teacher filled the stove with coal or wood. How is this different from your school?

7.2 Classrooms Were Different

One teacher taught all the grades. The younger children sat in front. The older children sat in back. How is this different from your classroom?

7.3 Children's Lives Were Different

Some children walked a long way to school. At recess, they rolled hoops for fun. Children who did not learn their lessons wore a dunce cap. How is this different from your life?

7.4 Classwork Was Different

Children used a hornbook. A hornbook is a one-page book. They wrote on slates with chalk. How is this different from your classwork?

Summary

Schools were different long ago. A schoolhouse had just one room. Children played different games. They used different tools in school.

From Buggies to Blastoff!

"Mister Bob" is 99 years old. He has seen many changes in travel. What was it like to travel long ago?

When I was a boy of 5, I lived on a farm. We had a horse and buggy. To go to the store, we had to hitch up the horse. Then we drove to town.

The road was dusty. The trip seemed to take forever. Going by horse and buggy was very slow. We never went much farther than town.

I took my first big trip when I was 15. I went by train. It was much faster than a horse and buggy. I was going to see the West.

I rode in a sleeping car. At night, the seats were turned into beds. Every morning, I looked out on a new place. I rode all the way from New York to California. I knew I would travel for the rest of my life.

When cars were invented, people gave up the horse and buggy. They all wanted cars. I got a car when I was 20. Then I could really go places.

Cars brought a new way of life. Roads got better. Towns changed. Drivers needed places to eat, sleep, and fill up the gas tank.

I drove all over the United States. At first, I camped out. Later, I stayed in motels.

I had my first plane ride when I was 30. The plane was tiny. But it was great to travel by air.

When I was 60, I flew to Japan. On a big jet, I could go halfway around the world in one day.

Travel keeps changing. Last week, on TV, I saw the space shuttle blast off. I know I will never travel into space. But maybe some day you will.

What Groups Do We Belong To?

New Ideas

school

family

community

8.1 We All Belong to Groups

A group has more than one person.

A group has something in common.

Groups can be big or small. What

groups can you name?

8.2 We Belong to School Groups

There are big and small groups at school. Our school is a big group. Our class is a smaller group. What other groups do we have at school?

8.3 We Belong to Family Groups

Families can be big or small.

A family can be two people. A family can be five people. How many people are in your family?

8.4 We Belong to Community Groups

There are many kinds of groups. Some groups play baseball. Some groups share a religion. What kinds of groups do you belong to?

Summary

We all belong to groups. We belong to school groups. We belong to family groups. We belong to community groups.

My Groups

We all belong to many groups. We learn from each group. What kind of things can we learn?

My name is Naomi Kashaya Jones. I live in June Lake, California. I belong to many groups. I have a few favorites. What about you?

My school is Mammoth Middle School. My favorite group at school is my sports group. I have learned how to play volleyball.

In a way, I have two family groups. One group is the family I live with.

Then there is the family I come from. I am an American Indian. My family is Miwok, Paiute, and Kashaya Pomo. Those are three American Indian groups, or tribes.

One of my grandmothers is a Kashaya Pomo. That is why I have the middle name Kashaya. It links me to the people in my past.

Are you part of a community group? I am in the Girl Scouts. We help our town. We pick up trash. We recycle cans and bottles.

I am also on a community ski team. I started when I was 6 years old. The ski team races every winter. We ski down the mountains near my town. Each year, I learn to ski a little better.

My next group is the one I love best. It is basket weavers. My family has four living basket weavers. I am one of them.

Basket weaving is an old American Indian craft. The women in my family have done this for years. Some of their baskets are in museums.

I learned to weave from my grandmother. I use plants that grow by the lake near my home. Weaving baskets is one more link to my past.

9

How Are Families Special?

New Ideas

family members

homes

activities

9.1 Families Are Special in Different Ways

Families can be big or small. They can live in the city or the country. They like to do different things. How is your family special?

9.2 Families Have Different Members

Some families have moms and dads.

Some families have brothers and sisters.

Some families have lots of cousins. Who

are the members of your family?

9.3 Families Live in Different Homes

Some families live in apartments. Some families live in houses. Some families live in mobile homes. Where does your family live?

9.4 Families Like Different Activities

Some families like to picnic in the park. Some families like to watch movies. Some families like to go fishing together. What does your family like to do?

Summary

Families are special in different ways. There are big families and small families. They live in different kinds of homes. They like to do different things.

Postcard Pen Pals

Families live in all kinds of different places. What makes each of these communities special?

The students in Room 1 have pen pals. They get postcards from all over.

The first one comes from Kayla in New York City. Her family lives in a tall building. From their window, they can see more tall buildings. Kayla walks to school. The streets are jammed with cars and trucks.

90

David sends a card from Hays, Kansas. His family lives on a farm. From their windows, they can see wide, flat fields.

David helps his dad in the barn. He also helps in the garden. He plants sunflowers and corn.

David rides the school bus to town. He has a pet dog, a pig, and a horse. He rides his horse on trails near his home.

Raja sends a card from San Jose, California. He says that the city spreads out for miles. Raja's mom and dad take the train to their office jobs.

Raja rides his bike to school. He can play outside most of the year. It never gets too cold, he says. The hills turn green in winter. In summer, he can get fresh fruit at roadside stands.

One card comes from Grace in Wakefield, Michigan. Her dad is a logger. He cuts trees to make lumber.

In July, Grace's family rents a cabin on a lake. The days are warm. Grace swims. She goes fishing in a rowboat.

But the winters bring deep snow. "Then I need a warm jacket," she writes. "And I have to watch for ice when I walk to school."

Luis lives near Moab, Utah. His family has a cattle ranch. Luis goes to school at home. His mom teaches him.

The desert can get very hot. Some days, Luis stays inside to keep cool.

Luis writes, "Not many people live around here. But people come to hike. They come to see the cliffs of red rock. They come to camp in the desert."

Jake writes from Seattle, Washington. He often walks to school in the rain. On clear days, he can see a snow-capped mountain.

Jake's dad has a fishing boat. He sells his catch at the fish market. They eat lots of fresh fish and crab.

Every day, Room 1 gets more postcards. What would you write to Room 1?

What Do Families Need and Want?

New Ideas

need

want

10.1 Families Need Food

Families need food to live. Food gives us energy. Food helps us grow. We eat some foods for breakfast. We eat other foods for lunch and dinner. What foods does your family eat?

10.2 Families Need Clothing

Clothing keeps us warm and dry. We wear coats in the winter. Clothing protects us from the sun. We wear hats in the summer. What kinds of clothing does your family wear?

10.3 Families Need Shelter

We all need a place to live. A home gives us a safe place to be.

Shelter protects families from sun, wind, rain, and snow. What kinds of shelters do families live in?

10.4 Families Want Things for Fun

Some children want new toys. Some families want other things for fun.

Things that we would like to have are called wants. Wants are not things we need to live. What kinds of things might families want for fun?

Summary

Families have needs and wants. They need food and clothing. They need shelter. Things that families don't need, but are nice to have, are called wants.

Meeting Wants and Needs

We all have wants. Let's say we want some popcorn. We can buy it at a store. But how did it get to the store?

Hi, kids! I am a piece of popcorn, and this is my story.

It all began with a farmer. He planted the seeds. He made sure they got water and sun.

Each seed grew into a tall corn stalk. Can you see the ears of corn? Each ear has many kernels. I was one of them.

The time came when the farmer had to sell his crop. He would use the money to pay for his family's needs. He would save some money to pay for their wants.

My days in the field had come to an end. It was time for workers and their big machines to take over. One machine picked the corn. Another machine cut the kernels from the cob.

A truck took us to a big plant. More machines cleaned and sorted us. The plant workers got us ready to sell at a store. I ended up in a bag with lots of other kernels.

Workers packed the bags into boxes. Other workers put the boxes on a truck. The truck driver drove to the store.

All these jobs are a way that people earn money to meet their needs.

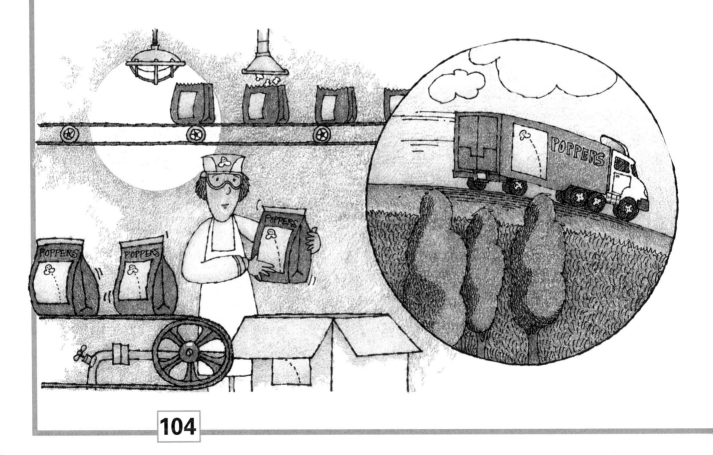

At the store, a worker put my bag on the shelf. A boy asked for a healthy snack. His mom picked up my bag. She gave money to the store clerk.

Working in a store is another way people can earn money to meet needs.

The family took me home. Soon, I would pop! I had come a long way from that farmer's field. Next time you eat popcorn, see if you can tell the story of where it came from.

How Do Family Members Care for Each Other?

New Ideas

help each other

share what you know

spend time together

11.1 Family Members Help Each Other

Families have chores to do. Adults buy the food. They cook the meals. Children can help set the table. They help wash the dishes. What chores do you do to help your family?

11.2 Family Members Share What They Know

Families talk and listen. Adults teach children how to do new things. Adults share books they like. Children share what they learn at school. What will you share with your family today?

11.3 Family Members Show Their Feelings

Families care about each other. They may show their love with hugs and kisses. They may use words to share their feelings. How do you show your family that you care about them?

11.4 Family Members Spend Time Together

Families work together. Families eat together. Families play together. What do you like to do with your family?

Summary

Family members help each other with chores. They share what they know. They show their feelings. They spend time together. These are all ways they show that they care.

Taking Care of Earth

Families take care of each other.

Earth is like a mother to all of us.

How can we take care of Earth?

Save water. Change the light bulbs. Walk, don't drive. Plant trees. Reduce trash. What's this all about?

Park School is getting ready for Earth Day. The children are making plans to take care of Earth's land, water, and air.

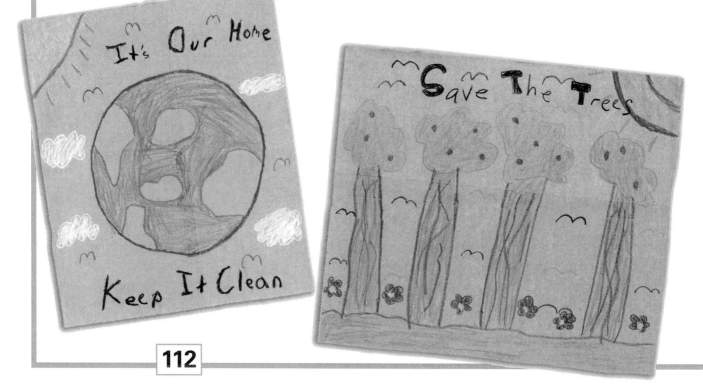

The children want Park School to be green. "Green" is a word we use to describe a place that is healthy and safe—for people and for Earth.

Schools can save water. Grade 1 checks all the drinking fountains. They find the ones that leak. These need to be fixed! They think of other ways to use less water.

A school uses a lot of electricity. Grade 2 learns about new kinds of light bulbs. They learn about turning out lights. They learn how we can get power from the sun. These are all ways to save energy.

Grade 3 learns about trees. Trees help keep the land and the air healthy. So Grade 3 plants trees. They want the school to be green outside, as well as inside.

Trash is a big problem for the world. There is too much of it! Grade 4 picks up trash on the school grounds. They talk about ways to make less trash.

Is Park School a green school now? It is greener than it was. Each little step helps. This is not a project for one day. At Park School, every day is Earth Day.

How Do Families Change?

New Ideas

change

grow

move

12.1 Families Change Over Time

People change over time. Parents change. Children change. Families change when people change. Can you think of one way your family has changed?

12.2 Family Members Grow Older

People look different as they grow older. Children grow taller. Grown-ups may get gray hair.

When children get older, they have different chores. They can do more things, too. What can you do now that you are older?

12.3 Families Grow Bigger

Families grow in different ways.
A new baby is born. A big sister gets
married. Parents adopt a child.

In what ways has your family grown
bigger? How many people are in your
family now?

12.4 Families Move to New Places

Some families move to new homes. They may need a bigger home. They may need a smaller home.

Some families move to new towns. They may be moving to a new job. Has your family changed where you live?

Summary

People grow older. Families change in size. Families move to new places. These are some ways that families change over time.

Old Family Pictures

Families change. Clothes change. Ways of life change. How do pictures show those changes?

I like to spend time at Grandma's house. She has books full of old pictures. It's fun to see how people used to live.

When Grandma was a little girl, she wore a dress most of the time. She liked to roller skate on the sidewalk.

Grandma says that housework was harder in the past. Doing the wash was a big job. Her mom had to put the wet clothes through a wringer. Then she took them outside. One by one, she hung them up to dry.

Today, my family has a washer and a dryer. Life is a lot easier with these.

Grandma loves music. When she was a girl, there were no CDs. There were no music downloads. What did she do?

She played records. Records were round and black, with a hole in the middle. People played them on a record player.

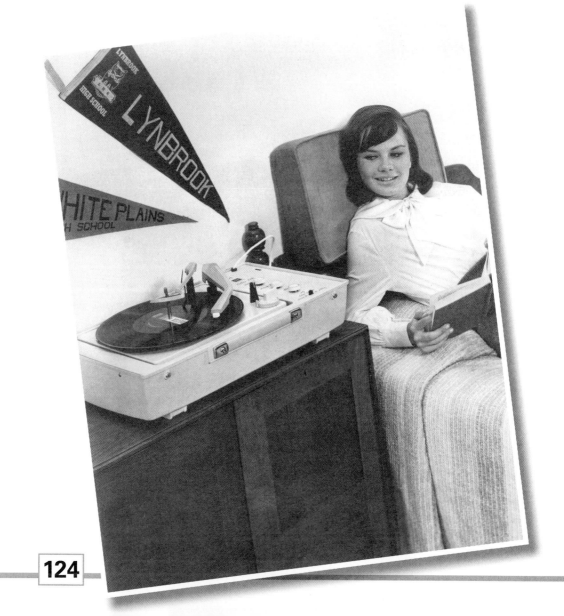

Grandma's dad worked for a newspaper. He had a typewriter. He used it to write his news stories.

Other people took pictures for the newspaper. Just look at the size of that old camera!

I like to take pictures, too. Some day my grandchildren will look at them. That way they can learn about my life.

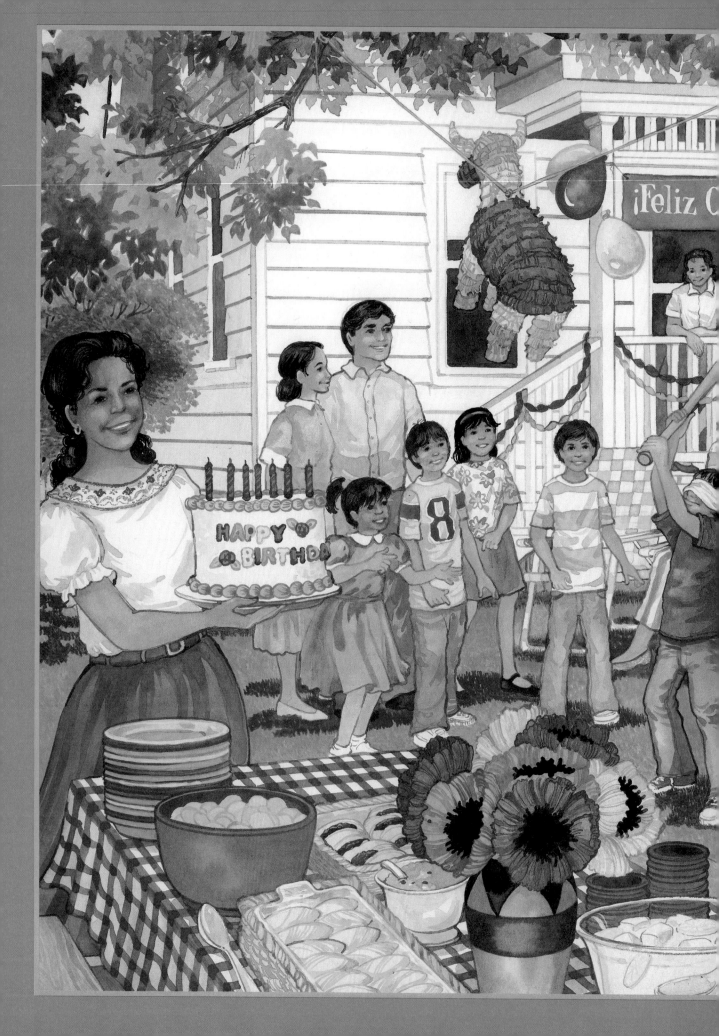

What Are Family Traditions?

New Ideas

tradition

celebrate

holiday

13.1 Traditions Are Special Ways of Doing Things

Some families eat special foods.

Some families wear special clothes.

Some families have a special way to

greet each other. What traditions does

your family have?

13.2 Adults Teach Children About Their Traditions

Some grandparents tell special stories. Some parents teach their children special games. Some parents teach their children how to make special things.

All of these things can be family traditions. Who teaches you about your family traditions?

13.3 Families Celebrate Special Days in Different Ways

Some families celebrate birthdays with balloons. Some families hang up a piñata. Some families sing a birthday song. How does your family celebrate your birthday?

13.4 Families Celebrate Different Holidays

Some families celebrate the Chinese Lantern Festival. Some families celebrate Thanksgiving. What special holidays can you name?

Summary

Traditions are special ways of doing things. Adults teach children about family traditions. Families celebrate special days in different ways. Families celebrate different holidays.

Traditions Around the World

People all around the world have their own traditions. Do you have any traditions like theirs?

PERU

Tito lives in Peru. His home is high in the Andes Mountains. He wears a wool cap and poncho to keep warm. Tito's friends wear clothes that look like his.

People wear all kinds of clothes. The clothes they wear can be a tradition. Do you have a tradition like that?

Midori lives in Japan. She is learning how to fold paper cranes. She will learn how to make frogs and boats, too. Her grandmother is teaching her.

An old legend says that if you make one thousand cranes, you will get what you wish for. Midori wants to try.

People make all kinds of things. Arts and crafts can be a tradition. Do you have a tradition like that?

Noor lives in India. His mother is a good cook. She uses lots of spices. She mixes them to make curry.

Spices come in many colors. Each one tastes different. Some of them are hot. Noor loves the spicy food of India.

People eat all kinds of food. A special kind of food can be a tradition. Do you have a tradition like that?

RUSSIA

Yuri lives in Russia. For fun, his family likes to play chess. Some of the best chess players in the world have come from Russia.

Chess is a hard game. Yuri is learning how to play. He must learn how to plan his chess moves.

People play all kinds of games. The games they play can be a tradition. Do you have a tradition like that?

Kofi lives in Ghana. The men in his village make their own drums.

Kofi's father is a good drummer. He taught his son. Now Kofi beats a drum. Other boys clap to the beat.

People like all kinds of music. Playing music can be a tradition. Do you have a tradition like that?

Grace lives in the United States. She loves parades. At the Veterans Day parade, Grace waves a flag.

Grace's aunt and her grandpa are both veterans. They fought for our country. On Veterans Day, we thank the people who fought for us.

People give thanks for many things. Giving thanks can be a tradition. Do you have a tradition like that?

UNITED STATES

What Do Good Neighbors Do?

New Ideas

neighbor

next door

neighborhood

14.1 Neighbors Are the People Who Live and Work Near Us

Some neighbors live next door to us.

Some neighbors live down the street.

Some neighbors work in stores nearby.

If we live in an apartment, we have

neighbors in the same building. If we

live in a house in the country, our

neighbors may be miles away. Who are

your neighbors?

14.2 Good Neighbors Help Each Other

Good neighbors do chores for someone who is sick. Good neighbors teach younger children how to play safely. Good neighbors take care of each other's pets. What do you do to help your neighbors?

14.3 Good Neighbors Get Along

Good neighbors wave when they see each other. Good neighbors ask, "How are you?"

Good neighbors spend time together. They may stop by your home to talk. Some neighbors have a block party every year. What do you do to get along with your neighbors?

14.4 Good Neighbors Take Care of Their Neighborhood

Good neighbors put away their bikes. They keep their homes clean. They pick up trash. They want their neighborhood to look nice. How do you take care of your neighborhood?

Summary

Neighbors are the people who live and work near us. Good neighbors help each other. Good neighbors get along. Good neighbors take care of their neighborhood.

The Apple Dumpling

Sometimes we want something that we don't have. How can our neighbors help?

Once upon a time, a woman wanted to make an apple dumpling. She had flour, butter, and spices, but she had no apples. "I have lots of plums," she said. "But plums are not apples. I need to trade. Maybe my neighbors can help."

The woman filled a basket with plums. Then she set off down the road.

The first neighbor she met had a
flock of geese. "I don't have apples,"
said the girl. "But I love plums. I'll trade
a bag of feathers for your plums."

Feathers will be easy to carry, the
woman thought. So she made the trade.

The next neighbor she met was a
pillow maker. "I need those feathers,"
the neighbor said. "I'll trade flowers
from my garden for your feathers."

The flowers smelled sweet—almost as sweet as an apple dumpling! So the woman made the trade.

Soon she met another neighbor on the road. He had a puppy in his arms. The man said, "I need a gift for my true love. I will trade my puppy for your flowers."

A puppy will be a good friend, the woman thought. So she made the trade.

The woman walked on. At the next house, she saw a lonely man. He was sitting under an apple tree. The woman took a long look at the apples. The man took a long look at her puppy. Can you guess what they did? Yes, they made the trade!

So the woman went home to make her apple dumpling. What would a person do without good neighbors?

Being a Good Citizen Through the Year

January

S M T W TH F S

● New Year's

● Martin Luther King Jr. Day

A new year begins! Think about the next 12 months. How can you be a good citizen all year long?

In January, you can honor Dr. Martin Luther King Jr.

Dr. King had a dream. He thought all people should have the same chances in life. He helped change laws that were not fair to African Americans. In this way, he worked for justice. Justice is fairness for everyone.

February is Black History Month.

Learn what these black heroes have done for our country.

Long ago, Harriet Tubman helped slaves escape to freedom.

Jackie Robinson played baseball. He opened the sport to black players.

We also have Presidents' Day this month. We call our first president, George Washington, the "father of our country."

Abraham Lincoln helped our country heal after it was torn apart by war.

March
S M T W TH F S
Women's History Month

In March, learn about these and other American women in history.

Sacajawea was an American Indian. She helped early Americans explore the West.

Susan B. Anthony spoke up to help women get the right to vote.

Helen Keller taught us to respect people who are deaf and blind.

In April, a great place to visit is Washington, D.C. That's the capital of our country.

You can join in the National Cherry Blossom Festival. The cherry trees, which bloom pink and white in the spring, were a gift to our country.

On your visit, you will see building like these.
The Capitol building is where our leaders meet to make laws.

This building honors Thomas Jefferson. He helped start our country long ago. You can see his face on the nickel.

Jefferson Memorial

In May, we celebrate Memorial Day. This is a day to remember the men and women who died in wars.

In a war, people fight one another. They fight to defend their countries. Many people die.

On Memorial Day, we put flowers on their graves. We thank them for keeping our country safe.

In June, we celebrate Flag Day. You can say the Pledge of Allegiance to the flag.

Some people say that Betsy Ross sewed the first flag of red, white, and blue.

The bald eagle is our national bird.

Our flag has 13 stripes. It has one star for each of the 50 states.

The flag is a symbol of our country. Our country has other symbols, too.

Uncle Sam wears red, white, and blue.

The fourth of July is the birthday of the United States. We call this Independence Day.

Thomas Jefferson wrote the Declaration of Independence. That was the start of our country more than 200 years ago.

People rang a big bell. We call it the Liberty Bell. It is a symbol of freedom. How will you celebrate? You could watch fireworks in the night sky.

In August long ago, Congress set up the National Park Service. It saves special places in our country for everyone to see.

August is a good month for a trip. You could visit one of our big parks. Yellowstone was our first national park.

Yellowstone Park

You could also visit the Lincoln Memorial. President Lincoln freed the slaves. One hot August day, Dr. King made a speech on the steps of this building. He spoke out for justice.

Lincoln Memorial

157

September

S M T W TH F S

Labor Day

Constitution Day

In September, on Labor Day, we honor everyone in our country who works—workers who make things, sell things, grow food, and help people.

We honor César Chávez. He stood up for farm workers. He helped give them a better life.

We can also celebrate Constitution Day. The Constitution sets up our country's government. It also protects our rights.

In October, we have Columbus Day.

Christopher Columbus was an explorer. Long ago, he sailed from Spain to North America. He met the American Indians who lived here.

People from all over the world still come to the United States. Today, the Statue of Liberty stands in New York harbor. It greets people coming to our country. It seems to say, "Welcome to a free land."

159

In November, we celebrate Veterans Day. You can fly the flag and thank our war heroes.

In this month, Americans vote for president. We can choose our leaders because our country is a democracy.

We can give thanks for this great country on Thanksgiving. This holiday started long ago. American Indians helped the Pilgrims who came to settle in America. In the fall, the Pilgrims gave thanks.

December

Washington Monument completed

One December, workers set the last stone in the Washington Monument. Now it stands tall in Washington, D.C.

It was built to honor our country's first president. Our capital city was named for him, too.

Each new president lives and works in our capital city. Do you know who lives in the White House today?

As the year ends, think about the things you can do to be a good citizen.

The Pledge of Allegiance

I pledge allegiance to the flag

of the United States of America

and to the Republic for which it stands,

one Nation under God,

indivisible,

with liberty and justice for all.

America

Words by Samuel Francis Ward
Based on an old tune

My country, 'tis of thee,

Sweet land of Liberty,

Of thee I sing.

Land where my fathers died,

Land of the pilgrims' pride,

From every mountainside,

Let freedom ring!

America the Beautiful

Words by Katharine Lee Bates
Melody by Samuel Ward

O beautiful, for spacious skies,

For amber waves of grain,

For purple mountain majesties

Above the fruited plain!

America! America!

God shed His grace on thee,

And crown thy good with

brotherhood

From sea to shining sea!

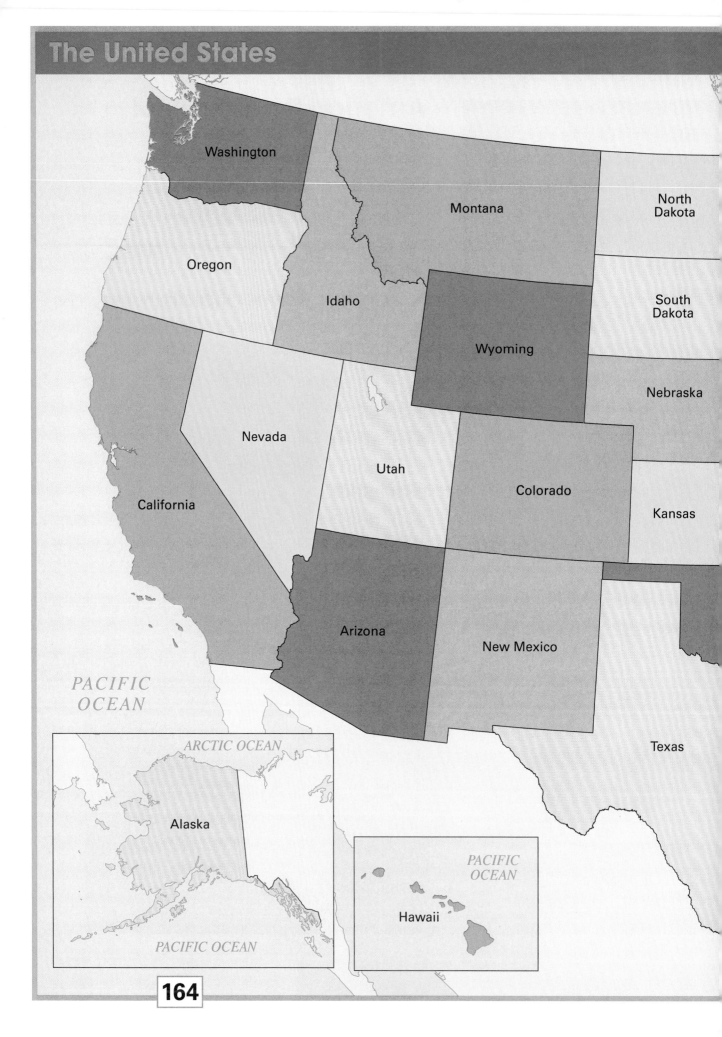

Washington

Oregon

Montana

North
Dakota

Idaho

South
Dakota

Wyoming

Nebraska

Nevada

Utah

Colorado

California

Kansas

Arizona

New Mexico

PACIFIC
OCEAN

ARCTIC OCEAN

Texas

Alaska

PACIFIC
OCEAN

Hawaii

PACIFIC OCEAN

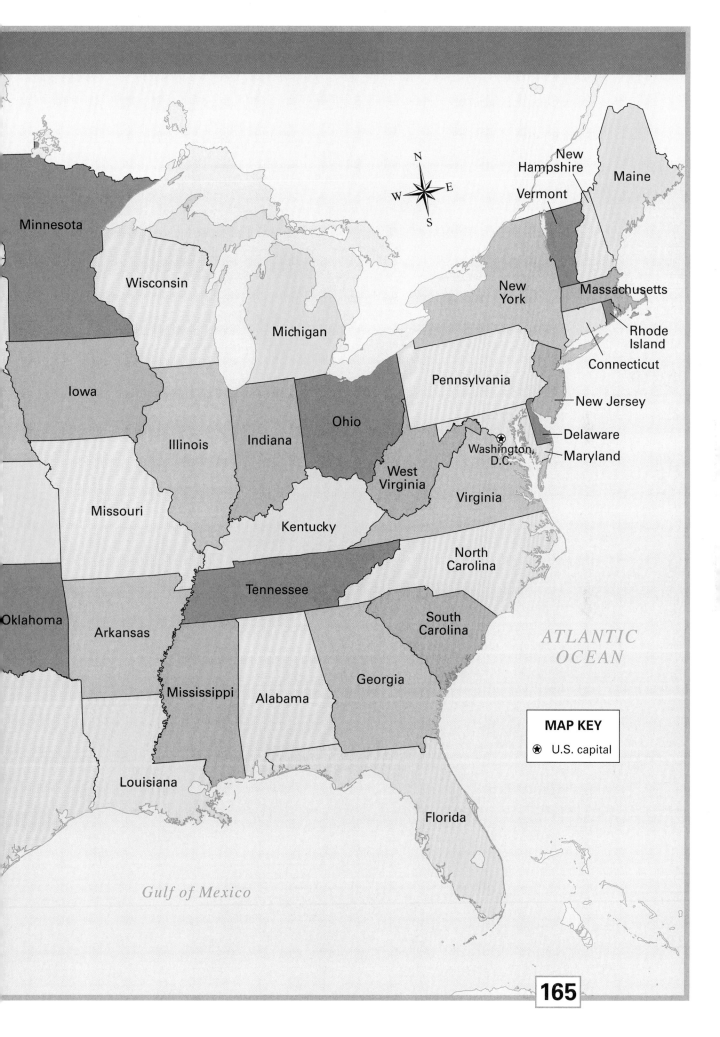

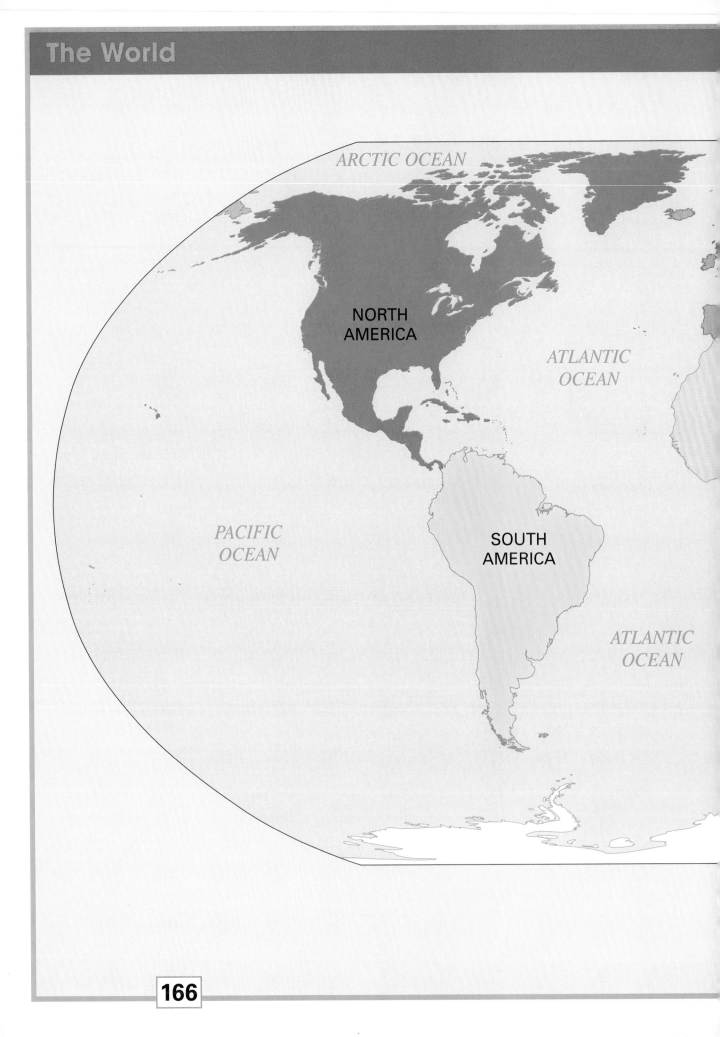

ARCTIC OCEAN

NORTH
AMERICA

ATLANTIC
OCEAN

PACIFIC
OCEAN

SOUTH
AMERICA

ATLANTIC
OCEAN

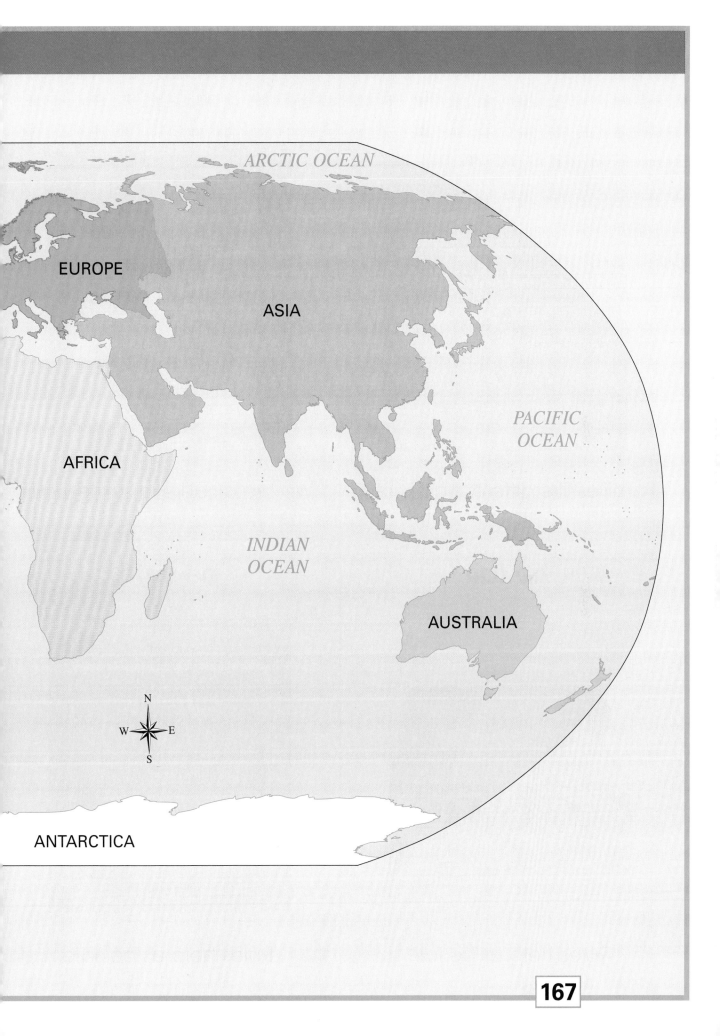

activities

Families like different activities.

alike

We are all alike in some ways.

be fair

Rules help us be fair.

be safe

Rules help us be safe.

celebrate

We celebrate special days.

change

People change over time.

community

People belong to
community groups.

compass rose

A compass rose shows
directions on a map.

custodian

The custodian cleans the school.

different

We are good at different things.

direction

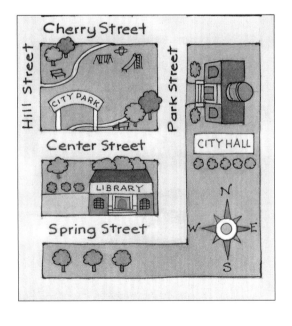

North is a direction on a map.

do our best

We do our best at school.

family

This family has four members.

family members

Family members share hugs.

get along

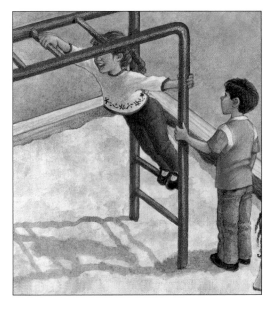

Taking turns helps us get along.

grow

Children grow older.

help each other

Family members help each other.

help others

We help others in our neighborhood.

holiday

The dragon dance is a Chinese holiday tradition.

homes

Families live in different kinds of homes.

hornbook

Children long ago learned
to read with a hornbook.

learn

We can learn from books.

listen

We listen to our friends.

long ago

Cars looked different
long ago.

map

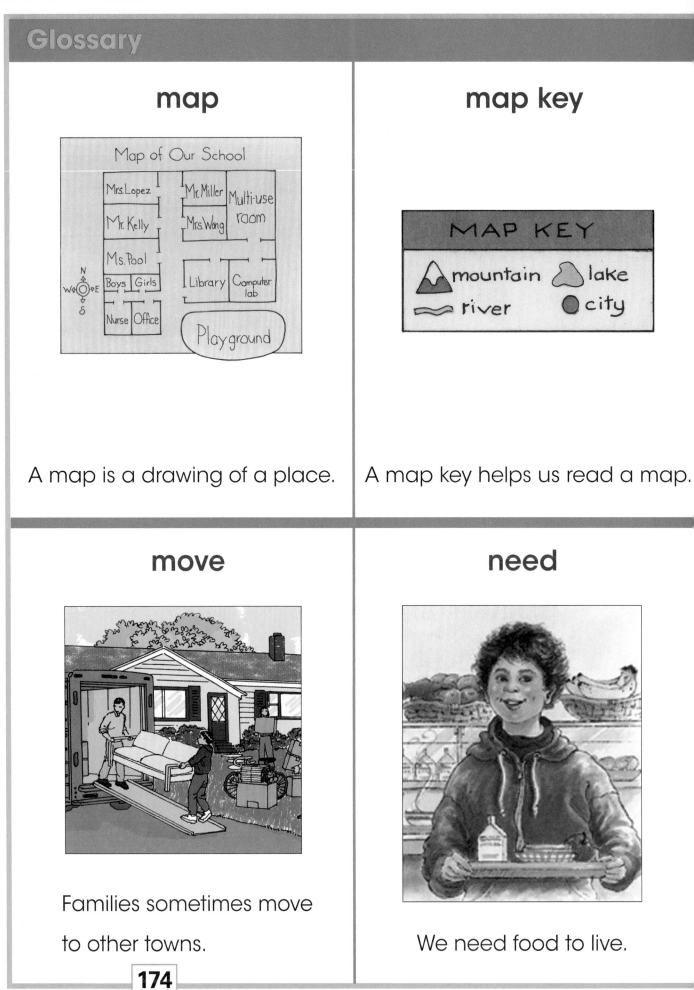

Map of Our School

Mrs. Lopez | Mr. Miller | Multi-use room
Mr. Kelly | Mrs. Wong
Ms. Pool
Boys | Girls | Library | Computer lab
Nurse | Office
Playground

A map is a drawing of a place.

map key

MAP KEY

mountain · lake
river · city

A map key helps us read a map.

move

Families sometimes move to other towns.

need

We need food to live.

neighbor

A good neighbor says "Hello."

neighborhood

A neighborhood may have a park.

next door

Some neighbors live next door to each other.

principal

The principal is a leader at school.

respect others

We respect others at school.

school

A school has classrooms.

schoolhouse

Long ago a schoolhouse had just one room.

secretary

The school secretary answers the telephone.

share

We share things in school.

share what you know

In a small group, you share what you know.

spend time together

We spend time together with family members.

symbol

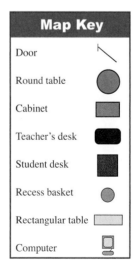

A map key shows each symbol used on a map.

take care of our things

We take care of our things.

take turns

We take turns at jump rope.

talk

We talk with family members.

teacher

A teacher helps us learn.

178

tradition

A piñata party can be a family tradition.

want

A want is not something we need to live.

Photographs

Chapter 10

98: Kevin Laubacher-Taxi/Getty Images **99:** RF/Digital Vision **100:** Buccina Studios/Getty Images **101:** Ken Chernus-RF-FPG/Getty Images

Chapter 11

108: Elyse Lewin/Getty Images **109:** SW Productions-RF/Getty Images **110:** Jim Cummins/Getty Images **111:** AJA Productions/Getty Images **113:** Jaimie D Travis/Getty Images **114 T:** David Wasserman-RF/Jupiter Images **114 B:** Jose Luis Pelaez, Inc./Corbis **115:** RF/Masterfile

Chapter 12

118: Tim Pannell/Corbis **119:** Andersen Ross-RF/Getty Images **120:** Stephen Simpson/Getty Images **121:** Ariel Skelley/Corbis **122 L:** George Marks/Getty Images **122 R:** Creatas-RF/SuperStock **123:** Culver Pictures, Inc./SuperStock **124:** The Granger Collection, New York **125 L:** Underwood and Underwood/Corbis **125 R:** Lambert Archive Photos/Getty Images

Chapter 13

128: B Tanaka/Getty Images **129:** Paul Chesley/Getty Images **130:** Elyse Lewin/Getty Images **131:** Kevin Fleming/Corbis **132:** Galen Rowell/Corbis **133:** Walter Hodges/Getty Images **134:** Nicolas DeVore/Getty Images **135:** Mina Chapman/Corbis **136:** Lineair/Peter Arnold **137 T:** AP Photo/Dima Gavrysh **137 B:** American Images, Inc./Getty Images

Chapter 14

140: Bob Torrez/Getty Images **141:** Don Smetzer/Getty Images **142:** Brooklyn Productions/Getty Images **143:** Richard Price/Getty Images

Being a Good Citizen

149 background: PSL Images-RF/Alamy **149 foreground:** Jon Feingersh-zefa/Corbis **150 BL:** Hulton Deutsch Collection/Corbis **150 BR:** Benjamin E. "Gene" Forte CNP/Corbis **151 TR:** Library of Congress **151 CR:** Bettmann/Corbis **151 BL:** Geoffrey Clements/Corbis **151 BR:** Library of Congress **152 TL:** US Mint **152 CR:** Corbis **152 BL:** Bettmann/Corbis **153 TR:** Visions LLC/Photolibrary **153 BR:** Bruce Dorrier/SuperStock **153 inset:** Don Farrall-RF/Alamy **154:** Associated Press **155 TR:** Joe Sohm-Visions of America/Getty Images **155 BL:** Arco Images GmbH/Alamy **156 TR:** RF/Getty Images **156 inset:** Corbis/SuperStock **156 B:** ThinkStock/SuperStock **157 T:** Shin Yoshino-Minden Pictures/Getty Images **157 T:** age fotostock/SuperStock **157 inset:** Time & Life Pictures/Getty Images **158 T:** Time & Life Pictures/Getty Images **158 B:** Todd Gipstein/Corbis **159 T:** Bettmann/Corbis **159 C:** The Granger Collection, New York **159 BL:** New York Public Library **160 TL:** Clayton Stalter-Journal Courier/The Image Works **160 BR:** Alison Miksch-Brand X/Corbis **161 BR:** Craig Aurness/Corbis **161 BL:** Steve Nudson/Alamy **162 T:** Steve Hamblin/Alamy **163 T:** Jose Fuste Raga/Corbis **163 B:** Craig Tuttle/Corbis

Credits

Art

Glossary

168 TL: Carol Newsome 168 TR: Doug Roy
168 BL: Susan Jaekel 168 BR: Doug Roy 169
TL: Dennis Hockerman 169 TR: DJ Simison
169 BL: Dennis Hockerman 170 TL: Gary
Undercuffler 170 TR: DJ Simison 170 BL:
Len Ebert 170 BR: Susan Jaekel 171 TL: DJ
Simison 171 TR: Susan Jaekel 171 BL: DJ
Simison 171 BR: DJ Simison 172 TL: Jane
McCreary 172 TR: Len Ebert 172 BL: Doug Roy
172 BR: Doug Roy 173 TL: Doug Roy 173 TR:
Susan Jaekel 172 BL: DJ Simison 173 BR: Len
Ebert 174 TL: Len Ebert 174 TR: Len Ebert
174 BL: Gary Undercuffler 174 BR: Susan
Jaekel 175 TL: Jane McCreary 175 TR: Carol
Newsome 175 BL: Len Ebert 175 BR: Gary
Undercuffler 176 TL: DJ Simison 176 TR:
Renate Lohmann 176 BL: Len Ebert 176 BR:
Gary Undercuffler 177 TL: Susan Jaekel 177
TR: Renate Lohmann 177 BL: Susan Jaekel
178 TL: DJ Simison 178 TR: DJ Simison 178
BL: Susan Jaekel 178 BR: Gary Undercuffler
179 TL: Dennis Hockerman 179 TR: Doug Roy

Artists represented by Ann Remen-Willis,
Artist Representative and Art Manager:

Len Ebert
Jon Goodell
Dennis Hockerman
Susan Jaekel
Renate Lohmann
Jane McCreary
Carol Newsome
Doug Roy
DJ Simison
Gary Undercuffler
Siri Weber Feeney